THE NEW MISSAL
EXPLAINING THE CHANGES

The New Missal

Explaining the Changes

NATIONAL CENTRE FOR LITURGY

First published 2011 by
Veritas Publications
7–8 Lower Abbey Street
Dublin 1
Ireland
publications@veritas.ie

ISBN 978 1 84730 272 4

A catalogue record for this book is available from the British Library.

Cover: Ancient mosaic inside the Church of the
Multiplication of the Loaves and the Fishes, Tabgha, Israel
Designed by Colette Dower, Veritas
Printed in the Republic of Ireland by Turners Printing Company Limited, Longford

CONTENTS

INTRODUCTION

The New Missal: Explaining the Changes has been put together by the National Centre for Liturgy to provide an account of the new edition of the Roman Missal and to offer an explanation of changes arising from it being a new translation.

It is written by Patrick Jones, with assistance from Moira Bergin, Julie Kavanagh and Liam Tracey.

The New Missal, as a study guide, takes up from *Celebrating the Mystery of Faith: A Guide to the Mass*, which followed the publication of the new edition of the *General Instruction of the Roman Missal* in 2005. The contents of this book will guide the reader or study group on aspects of the new edition of the Roman Missal and the textual changes, as guided by the 2001 Instruction on translation, *Liturgiam authenticam*. Attention is given primarily to changes in the texts of the congregation, though aspects of the Eucharistic Prayer are treated in chapters 11 and 12. Chapters, however, vary in length and in style, sometimes structured as an overview and sometimes in more detail. Some of the material has appeared in *Intercom*, a pastoral and liturgical resource magazine published by Veritas Communications, an agency of the Irish Bishops' Commission on Communications.

The National Centre for Liturgy records its thanks to Veritas Publications and Colette Dower for design and typesetting. It also acknowledges the help given generously and efficiently by the International Commission on English in the Liturgy.

ABBREVIATIONS

SC   Vatican II, The Constitution on the Sacred Liturgy, *Sacrosanctum concilium* (4 December 1963)

GIRM   *General Instruction on the Roman Missal*, including Adaptations for the Dioceses of Ireland (2005)

CDWDS   Congregation of Divine Worship and the Discipline of the Sacraments

ICEL   International Commission on English in the Liturgy

CHAPTER ONE

THE NEW EDITION OF THE ROMAN MISSAL

On 25 March 2010, the Congregation for Divine Worship and the Discipline of the Sacraments gave its recognitio or approval of the new English translation of the Roman Missal, the book of prayers used at Mass. A presentation edition was given to Pope Benedict XVI on 28 April 2010. The Irish Bishops at their general meeting in June 2010 noted the completion of this stage of a translation project that began with the publication of a new edition of the Latin Missale Romanum in March 2002. The text in its new translation was received by Presidents of English-speaking Bishops' Conferences towards the end of August along with the decree authorising publication and use. Some editing continued and a copy of the Order of Mass and its music was received in mid-November 2010, with the rest of the material being received just before Christmas 2010. Various aspects of publication have been attended to and the full implementation of the new Missal, as the June 2010 statement of the Bishops said, is 'towards the end of 2011'.

The new edition of the Missal replaces the book we have used since 16 March 1975. Though the vernacular had been introduced into the Mass on the First Sunday of Lent 1965, the Eucharistic Prayer remained in Latin until 1 December 1968. The introduction of the vernacular was well received and has proved to be one of the great blessings of the reform and renewal of the Church's liturgy. The vernacular has become, in the words of Pope Paul VI, 'the praying voice of the Church', and the Missal we have used for thirty-five years has enabled this to happen.

Now we move towards a new edition of the Missal and a new translation.

WHY A NEW EDITION OF THE ROMAN MISSAL?

The new edition is necessitated by the publication of a new Latin edition in 2002, amended and reprinted in 2008. This is the typical edition (*editio typica*) which is used for translation into the vernacular. The Missal we have been using is a translation of the first Latin edition of 1970. (A second Latin edition was published in 1975, with some extra Mass texts, for example, the Dedication of a Church and an Altar, and Mary, Mother of the Church, and some paragraphs on the role of the acolyte and reader in the introductory documentation, replacing what had been said about the sub-deacon.)

A new edition will contain what is in the Latin editions of 1970 and 1975 and the additional material added since then. It will also be in a new translation according to more recent norms and guidelines on translation.

WHAT IS THE ROMAN MISSAL?

The early Church used the principle, *lex orandi, lex credendi* (the law of prayer [is] the law of belief) and was conscious of the need for orthodoxy and good practice. The prayers used in the liturgy were collected into *libelli* or booklets, the most important of which is the *Verona Sacramentary* from the late sixth century, originally a collection of prayers used in the papal liturgies. Larger collections developed into 'sacramentaries', the best known being the *Gelasian Sacramentary* and its several variants. It is named after the late-fifth century Pope Gelasius but dates from the mid-eighth century. The term 'sacramentary' is well known as it has been used for many years in the United States as the title of what we have simply called the Missal. Many of the prayers of these ancient books are still used today.

The term 'missal' is used of those liturgical books which contained the prayers, readings, chants and rubrics, or instructions, for the celebration of Mass. They developed in the monasteries in the twelfth and thirteenth centuries and soon became the Mass book for priests in parishes. The first book with the title *Missale Romanum* dates from 1474. The most famous edition is that of 1570, after the Council of Trent. This Missal, often called the *Missal of Pope Pius V*, was promulgated for obligatory use throughout the Roman Rite. *The Tridentine Mass.*

Various editions have been published since 1570, noting here the 1962 edition, sometimes called the *Missal of Pope John XXIII*. This Missal includes the changes made in the liturgies of Holy Week in 1956 and is the last edition before the Second Vatican Council. It is the Missal that is used in the Extraordinary Form of the Roman Rite, often called the Tridentine Mass.

The Missal of 1970, the *Missal of Pope Paul VI*, contains the revisions mandated by the Second Vatican Council. *– e. g. set out in "Sacrosanctum Concilium".*

WHAT IS NEW IN THE MISSAL?

The new English language Missal is a translation of the third edition of the Latin *Missale Romanum*, published in 2002, with an amended reprint in 2008. It contains what is in the Missal in use since 1975 but with many additions. However, it omits texts that are not in the Latin Missal, most notably, the alternative Opening Prayers for Sundays which were composed for the 1975 Missal. The additions include:

- Three additional Eucharistic Prayers, that is, the two Eucharistic Prayers for Reconciliation, introduced for the Holy Year of 1975, and the Eucharistic Prayer for Masses for Various Needs, which was approved for Ireland in 1995;
- Some Mass texts included in the second edition of the Latin Missal in 1975;
- Prayers over the People for the days of Lent, reviving an old liturgical tradition;
- *removal of the 'nature as a "rending out"'* — New formularies for the dismissal which Pope Benedict XVI requested in order to show the link between the celebration of the Eucharist and living the Eucharist;
- Masses for over twenty feasts that have been placed on the General Calendar since 1975, for example, St Maximilian Kolbe, St Teresa Benedicta of the Cross (Edith Stein), St Pius of Pietrelcina (Padre Pio), Our Lady of Guadalupe;
- The Patrons of Europe, which are noted;
- Though not in the Latin Missal, our National Proper, that is, the prayers for Masses of our Irish Calendar, placed in sequence within the General Calendar. These prayers and also readings where given have been published as the *National Proper for Ireland* in 2009;
- some extra Masses of the Blessed Virgin Mary, mostly taken from the *Collection of Masses of the Blessed Virgin Mary* published in 1987;
- some extra Mass texts for Votive Masses and Masses for Various Needs and Occasions;
- the extended Vigil of Pentecost;
- the inclusion of music in place where it is used rather than in appendices;
- the revised *General Instruction of the Roman Missal*. This was published in 2005.

A MORE DETAILED DESCRIPTION OF SOME OF THE NEW MATERIAL IN THE NEW EDITION

Eucharistic Prayers

The new edition of the Missal has seven Eucharistic Prayers. The 1975 Missal contains four Eucharistic Prayers, that is, the Roman Canon, which had been our one Eucharistic Prayer for over 1,500 years, and three Eucharistic Prayers composed for the new Latin Missal of 1970. The new edition of the Missal will contain these four Prayers and three more approved since 1975. The four Eucharistic Prayers of the 1975 Missal are placed in the Order of Mass and the three new Eucharistic Prayers are added in an appendix to the Order of Mass. More accurately they are only new in being included in the Missal as these Eucharistic Prayers have been in use for some years. Inclusion in the Missal makes for more frequent use.

- *Eucharistic Prayers for Reconciliation* were issued for the Holy Year of 1975 and the texts were prepared to illustrate aspects of reconciliation, which was the theme of the Year and may be the object of thanksgiving. The Missal suggests their use during Lent and in Masses in which the mystery of reconciliation is conveyed in a special way, as in several Masses for Various Needs and Occasions, for example, for promoting harmony, for reconciliation, for the preservation of peace and justice, in time of war or civil disturbance, for the forgiveness of sins and for charity, and in Votive Masses of the mystery of the Cross, of the Eucharist, and of the Most Precious Blood.

  Although these Eucharistic Prayers are provided with a proper Preface, they may also be used with other Prefaces that refer to penance and conversion, for example, the Prefaces of Lent.

- *Eucharistic Prayer for use in Masses for Various Needs* has its origins in a Eucharistic Prayer approved for the Swiss Synod of 1974. Other countries sought and received permission to use it. When a Latin *editio typica* was made available, an English translation was made. This interim translation was approved for Ireland in May 1995. A new translation is included in the new edition of the Missal.

  This Eucharistic Prayer has four Prefaces and corresponding intercessions and the Missal publishes the Eucharistic Prayer in four complete forms. The Eucharistic Prayer is given four themes and examples of use with Masses for Various Needs and Occasions are given:

  I. The Church on the Path of Unity – suggested with Mass formularies such as: for the Church, the Pope, the Bishop, a Council or Synod, for Priests, for Ministers of the Church, and for a spiritual or pastoral gathering;
  II. God guides his Church along the Way of Salvation – suggestions include with Mass formularies such as: for the Church, vocations, the family, religious, etc.;
  III. Jesus, the Way to the Father – appropriately used with Mass formularies such as: for the evangelisation of peoples, for those in public office, for the progress of peoples, etc.;
  IV. Jesus, who went about doing good – appropriately used with Mass formularies such as: for refugees and exiles, in time of famine, for the sick and dying, and in any need.

Prayers over the People

These prayers developed as early as the fourth century as part of the formal ending of the Mass when the blessing was given and the people were dismissed. From the seventh century they were retained in the Mass during Lent. The 1975 Missal contains twenty-six prayers which can be used at any occasion. Increased to twenty-eight in the new Missal, they are placed with Solemn Blessings at the end of the Order of Mass.

In restoring the old Roman tradition, each day of Lent is also given a Prayer over the People. The Prayer for Ash Wednesday at the beginning of Lent is:

> Pour out a spirit of compunction, O God,
> on those who bow before your majesty,
> and by your mercy may they merit the rewards you promise
> to those who do penance.
> Through Christ our Lord.

New formularies for the Dismissal

In the Latin Missal, the concluding rites have included a dismissal of the people with the words, *Ite, missa est*. These words have given us the most common name for the Eucharist, the Mass. The phrase can be translated as a dismissal, such as, 'Go, you are sent', or that the Mass has ended or it can refer to mission. This was noted at the Synod of Bishops held in 2005 and in Pope Benedict XVI's post-synodal document, *Sacramentum Caritatis*. He wrote, 'These few words succinctly express the missionary nature of the Church. The People of God might be helped to understand more clearly this essential dimension of the Church's life, taking the dismissal as a starting-point'. In addition to 'Go forth, the Mass is ended', the 2008 reprint of the *Missale Romanum* added the following:

> Go and announce the Gospel of the Lord.
>
> Go in peace, glorifying the Lord by your life.
>
> Go in peace.

New Feasts

Feasts, using the word in a general way, are classified by their importance and are called solemnities, feasts and memorials. Solemnities are the days of greatest importance and have their own readings and proper prayers. Several solemnities have their own Vigil Mass, celebrated in the evening of the preceding day. Feasts are of the second order and also have their own readings and prayers. Memorials are of the third order and are observed in combination with the celebration of the weekday on which they occur. Usually, when the memorial is classed as obligatory, the Collect of the memorial, the Prayer over the Offerings and the Prayer after Communion are said with the readings of the day. Many memorials are classed as optional and their observance is at the discretion of those who are celebrating the Mass of the day.

In addition to the feast of St Teresa Benedicta of the Cross (Edith Stein), the following new saints are included as obligatory memorials:

* St Maximilian Kolbe (14 August), who died in the concentration camp of Auschwitz in 1941;
* Ss Andrew Kim Taegŏn, Paul Chŏng Hasang and Companions (20 September), 103 Korean martyrs, 1839–1867;
* St Pius of Pietrelcina (Padre Pio) (23 September), died 1968, Capuchin friar, stigmatist, confessor, friend of all who suffer;
* Ss Andrew Dung-Lac and Companions (24 November), 117 Vietnamese martyrs of seventeenth, eighteenth and nineteenth centuries canonised in 1988.

The following Saints are included as optional memorials:

* St Josephine Bakhita (8 February) – brought as a slave from her native Sudan to Italy. Later became a nun, died 1947;
* St Adalbert of Prague (23 April) – bishop of Prague and later a missionary among the Prussians. Martyred 997;
* St Louis Marie Grignon de Montfort (28 April) – priest and great promoter of praying the Rosary;
* Ss Christopher Magallánes and Companions (21 May) – twenty-five Mexican martyrs executed in 1927;
* St Rita of Cascia (22 May) – after her husband's murder, entered the Augustinian convent in Cascia;
* Ss Augustine Zhao Rong and Companions (9 July) – 120 Chinese martyrs, many executed during the Boxer Risings;
* St Apollinaris (20 July) – second century bishop of Classis in Italy and martyr;
* St Charbel Makhlūf (24 July) – Lebanese monk and hermit;
* St Peter Julian Eymard (2 August) – founder of the Blessed Sacrament Fathers, died 1868;
* St Peter Claver (9 September) – Spanish Jesuit priest who worked with the slaves in Colombia;
* Ss Lawrence Ruiz and Companions (28 September) – sixteen Japanese martyrs, died 1633–1637;

- St Catherine of Alexandria (25 November) – martyred in 310 at Alexandria. Her body is venerated at the monastery on Mount Sinai;
- St Juan Diego Cuahtlatoatzin (9 December) – saw the vision of Our Lady of Guadalupe in December 1571.

Some Days of Devotion are added, as optional memorials:

- The Most Holy Name of Jesus (3 January). 'He was called Jesus, the name given by the angel before he was conceived in the womb [of Mary]' (Lk 2:21);
- Our Lady of Fatima (13 May) – recalls the apparitions of the Blessed Virgin Mary to the three children in 1917 with the message of doing penance and praying the Rosary;
- The Most Holy Name of Mary (12 September) – an observance restored to the General Calendar honouring the Blessed Virgin Mary under her name;
- Our Lady of Guadalupe (12 December) – the patron of the Americas. This memorial recalls the apparitions in December 1531 on Tepayac Hill, near Mexico city;

and an additional title:

- Divine Mercy (2nd Sunday of Easter) – added to the Second Sunday of Easter by Pope John Paul II in 2000 at the canonisation of St Faustina, who promoted devotion to the divine mercy of Jesus.

The Immaculate Heart of Mary is raised to an obligatory memorial, if the date, the day after the solemnity of the Sacred Heart of Jesus, is available.

Patrons of Europe

- St Benedict. In 1964, Pope Paul VI declared Benedict patron of Europe, calling him 'messenger of peace, architect of European unity and mentor of its civilisation, above all herald of the Christian religion and father of Western monasticism.' He founded the monastery of Monte Cassino where he died in 547. Feast: 11 July.
- Ss Cyril and Methodius. In 1980, Pope John Paul II declared them patrons. They lived in the ninth century and were brothers from Thessalonica, Greece. They are honoured as the apostles of the Slavic people. They preached the gospel in Moravia, using their own translation of the Scriptures and the liturgy in the local language. These translations into Slavonic were based on an alphabet they invented, now called Cyrillic. Feast: 14 February.

Three new patrons were announced by Pope John Paul II in 1999.

- St Bridget of Sweden, 1303–1373 – a devoted wife and mother of eight children. After being widowed, she founded a religious order, known as the Bridgettines. She is remembered for her asceticism, her dedication to reform within the Church and her lifelong mystical experience of Christ's passion. Feast: 23 July.
- St Catherine of Siena – born in Siena in 1347, died 1380. She entered the Dominican Order as a young girl and became an influential leader, working for the reconciliation of Church and state and the reform of the Papacy. Though unable to write, she is remembered as a spiritual teacher, mystic and reformer of religious life. Feast: 29 April.
- St Teresa Benedicta of the Cross (Edith Stein) – born in 1891 into a prosperous Jewish family in Breslau, Germany. She was baptised into the Catholic Church in 1922, taking the name Teresa, and later became a Carmelite nun in Cologne, taking the name Benedicta. She died in the gas chambers of Auschwitz in 1942. She was canonised in 1999. Feast: 9 August.

National Proper

The National Proper for Ireland, as approved by the Congregation for Divine Worship and the Discipline of the Sacraments, was published as an interim supplement to the Roman Missal in 2009 and is incorporated into the new edition of the Roman Missal.

The National Calendar, revised and approved in 1972, had only five observances, including one solemnity (St Patrick) and four feasts (St Brigid, St Columba (Colm Cille), All the Saints of Ireland and St Columban). In 1976, a sixth observance was added with the inclusion of the feast of the then newly canonised St Oliver Plunkett.

In the work of a revision of the National Proper in the mid-1990s, a fuller calendar was proposed. The Congregation for Divine Worship and the Discipline of the Sacraments (CDWDS) confirmed the proposed Proper Calendar of Saints for Ireland in October 1998. This revised Calendar allows the celebration of Irish saints in the national calendar rather than just as diocesan celebrations. This revision, therefore, allows for a greater Irish identity to be given to the Calendar. It has one solemnity (St Patrick), three feasts (St Brigid, St Columba, All Saints of Ireland) and memorials which commemorate diocesan patrons and others. There are seven obligatory memorials: St Ita, St Kevin, Bl. Irish Martyrs, St Oliver Plunkett, St Ciaran, St Malachy and St Columban. Additions to the Calendar include Saints Fursa, Gobnait, David, Aengus, Enda, Davnet, Moninne, Willibrord, Aidan of Lindisfarne and Fergal.

As a general norm, solemnities and feasts are regarded as exceptional, with full Mass prayer texts and readings. The Solemnity of St Patrick has been given a three-year cycle of readings. This solemnity and the three feasts also have proper Prefaces and Solemn Blessings. The obligatory memorials are given a Collect, Prayer over the Offerings, Prayer after Communion as well as their own entrance and communion antiphons. The optional memorials only have a Collect.

The Collect for the feast of All the Saints of Ireland (6 November) is:

> Lord God,
> as we celebrate the power of the Gospel
> that you displayed in the Saints of our land,
> work for us, we pray, new wonders of your grace:
> that the faith may grow stronger among us,
> and true charity bind us in peace.
> Through our Lord Jesus Christ, your Son,
> who lives and reigns with you in the unity of the Holy Spirit,
> one God, for ever and ever.

The Calendar for Ireland is given in Appendix I (p. 57).

CHAPTER TWO

A NEW TRANSLATION OF THE MISSAL
An overview of the journey to a new translation

The new edition of the Roman Missal is published in a new translation. Here a short explanation of how we have journeyed to a new translation is given, beginning with a comparison of a prayer in the old and new editions of the Missal.

AN EXAMPLE OF TWO TRANSLATIONS

On 28 November 2010, First Sunday of Advent, with the translation that we have used since 1975, the Collect read:

> All-powerful God,
> increase our strength of will for doing good
> that Christ may find an eager welcome at his coming
> and call us to his side in the kingdom of heaven,
> where he lives and reigns with you and the Holy Spirit,
> one God, for ever and ever.

At the beginning of Advent, 27 November 2011, the prayer in its new translation reads:

> Grant your faithful, we pray, almighty God,
> the resolve to run forth to meet your Christ
> with righteous deeds at his coming,
> so that, gathered at his right hand,
> they may be worthy to possess the heavenly kingdom.
> Through our Lord Jesus Christ, your Son,
> who lives and reigns with you in the unity of the Holy Spirit,
> one God, for ever and ever.

The prayer in Latin reads:

> Da, quaesumus, omnipotens Deus,
> hanc tuis fidelibus voluntatem,
> ut, Christo tuo venienti iustis operibus occurentes,
> eius dexterae sociati,
> regnum mereantur possidere caeleste.
> Per Dominum.

The prayer, a prayer after communion from seventh-century sacramentaries, was placed in the Latin Missal after the Second Vatican Council as the first Collect of Advent. A more detailed commentary is given in Appendix II (p. 59).

This prayer illustrates several aspects of the new translation. The 1975 translation has not included all words and phrases of the Latin. With our new translation, we pray that we, running with righteous or good deeds to Christ, 'at his coming', may be gathered at his right hand and be worthy to possess the kingdom of heaven. There are more words because they are in the Latin. It is a single sentence as the Latin collects are. A prayer of more words in a single sentence often will necessitate prior familiarity. But we cannot argue against being prepared!

Note also the clear biblical resonances since our liturgical prayer is rooted in the Bible. It has been a special concern of those who worked on the translation to express well these biblical references and resonances. Here, 'to run' echoes several references in St Paul (see 1 Cor 9:24-26, Gal 2:2, 5:7, also Heb 12:1). In Advent, while we wait, we also hasten to meet Christ in glory. The prayer also reminds us that those on God's right hand are those who inherit the kingdom (Mt 25:34).

THE USE OF THE VERNACULAR

The Second Vatican Council (1962–1965) and, in particular, the Constitution on the Sacred Liturgy, extended the horizons for the use of the vernacular in the liturgy, that is, for us the use of Irish and English in the Mass and other liturgies. Though the Constitution said that this would apply to the readings and instructions and to some prayers and chants in the first place, within a very short period all our liturgies were celebrated in the vernacular. Here in Ireland we introduced the first stage of the use of the vernacular into the Mass on 4 March 1965, First Sunday of Lent. Less than four years later, on 1 December 1968, First Sunday of Advent, the remaining part of the Mass, the Eucharistic Prayer, was said in the vernacular.

The task of translation was entrusted to the International Commission on English in the Liturgy (ICEL), established at a meeting of representatives of Bishops' Conferences in English-speaking countries on 17 October 1963, several weeks before the solemn promulgation of the Constitution on the Liturgy. A move to using the vernacular was clearly on the way.

COMME LE PRÉVOIT

The Missal, revised in the light of the Second Vatican Council, was published in its Latin typical edition in 1970. ICEL began its work of translation, but by then an 'instruction on the translation of liturgical texts for celebrations with a congregation' had been issued on 25 January 1969 by the Roman *Concilium*, the commission entrusted with the implementation of the reform indicated by the Constitution on the Liturgy. This document was first drafted in French, hence its title *Comme le prévoit*, and sent to each of the major language commissions, including ICEL. They were able to include illustrations appropriate to the genius of their language. It advised translators to give first consideration to translating the meaning and to see the 'unit of meaning', not in the individual word but the whole passage. This approach is known as 'dynamic equivalence', as distinct from a literal, word-for-word approach or 'formal equivalence' or 'formal correspondence.' *Comme le prévoit* stressed that translation had also to be judged in terms of being an act of communication to a particular congregation. The language should be in 'common usage', though 'worthy of expressing the highest realities'.

The Collect of the First Sunday of Advent, as in the 1975 Missal, is an example of translation according to *Comme le prévoit*.

LITURGIAM AUTHENTICAM

This Collect in the new translation is according to the norms of *Liturgiam authenticam*. This is a document issued by the Congregation for Divine Worship and the Discipline of the Sacraments (CDWDS) on 21 March 2001 and in effect on 25 April of that year. It is the 'Fifth Instruction for the Right Implementation of the Constitution on the Liturgy' since the Second Vatican Council. It calls for an examination of the translation in use and directs that 'the original text, insofar as possible, must be translated integrally and in the most exact manner, without omissions or additions in terms of their content, and without paraphrases or glosses' (20). The translation is to follow the Latin structure: 'the connection between various expressions, manifested by subordinate and relative clauses, the ordering of words, and various forms of parallelism, is to be maintained as completely as possible in a manner appropriate to the vernacular language' (57). The Instruction gives several specific directives, for example, *et cum spiritu tuo* to be translated 'and with your spirit'; masculine language to be used for God and the persons of the Trinity. While repeating what was also in *Comme le prévoit* that the language should be 'easily understandable', it states that translations need to preserve the 'dignity, beauty and doctrinal precision' of the Latin and should show a 'sacred style'.

A more detailed summary of the Instruction appears in Appendix III (p. 61) and the full Instruction is available on www.vatican.va.

A more detailed commentary, *Ratio translationis for the English Language*, was issued by the CDWDS in 2007.

WORSHIP – GOD'S GIFT IN HUMAN VOICE

As we look at different prayers in the Mass we will see the differences between what we have been saying for thirty-five years and what we will have from the end of 2011. An important element for the translators has been to make clear the connection between the prayers and Scriptures, as can be seen in the example of the Advent Collect on page 15. Also, the same example shows how the new translation follows the Latin words and sentence structure more closely. Above all, the new translation will remind us that in worship we are in God's presence, that we are on holy ground with God, that worship is God's gift that we return with human voice and body.

CHAPTER THREE

THE ROMAN MISSAL
An overview of content

An overview of the contents of the Roman Missal.

The Missal is the prayer book used at Mass. As well as prayers, it contains the chants and music and the rubrics or directions for celebration. The introduction includes:

- Apostolic Constitution of Pope Paul VI promulgating the Roman Missal as revised by decree of the Second Vatican Council. Its first document, the Constitution on the Sacred Liturgy, established the basis for a general revision of the Missal

- Decrees authorising the three editions of the Missal and the decree specifically for Ireland, authorising the use of the new edition

- General Instruction of the Roman Missal (GIRM): the principle introductory document for the Missal. It is both a 'how' and 'why' document in that it explains the way Mass is celebrated but also the understanding that lies behind it. The new edition that is part of the new edition of the Missal was issued in July 2000 ahead of its inclusion in the Latin Missal published in 2002. Its English translation for Ireland was published in 2005

- Universal Norms for the Liturgical Year and the General Roman Calendar: completing the front material and offering an understanding of the Liturgical Year and how it is arranged through the Calendar.

The several sections of the Roman Missal, its prayers, chants and rubrics, include:

- Order of Mass: the central part of the Missal and the part which is used at every Mass. It contains:
  - ❋ the introductory rites;
  - ❋ an outline of the Liturgy of the Word, though not the readings which are found in the Lectionary. The Nicene and Apostles' Creed are also given;
  - ❋ the Liturgy of the Eucharist, in which we find the seven Eucharistic Prayers approved for Ireland and over 100 prefaces, that is, the variable first part of the Eucharistic Prayer;
  - ❋ the concluding rites

- Proper of Time: contains the prayers for Masses within the seasons, Advent, Christmas, Lent, the Easter Triduum, Easter time and also for the Sundays of Ordinary Time. At the end of this section is found the Masses for the Solemnities of the Lord during Ordinary Time, that is, Trinity Sunday, the Body and Blood of Christ (Corpus Christi), the Sacred Heart of Jesus and Christ the King

- Proper of Saints: contains the prayers used on the feasts of the Saints, from January to December. In the new edition the Irish saints are included in the sequence of the General Calendar

- Commons: has the prayers for Masses in honour of the Blessed Virgin Mary, the saints and the Dedication of a Church when these celebrations do not have their own proper prayers

- Ritual Masses: has the prayers used in the various rituals, both when celebrated within Mass and outside of Mass, including at the sacraments of Christian Initiation, including the Baptism of Children, Anointing of the Sick, Viaticum, Holy Orders, Marriage, Blessing of an Abbot or an Abbess, Religious Profession, the institution of Lectors and Acolytes and for the Dedication of a Church and an Altar

- Masses and Prayers for Various Needs and Occasions: contains prayers for needs and occasions given in three groups, for the Holy Church, for Civil Needs and for Various Intentions

- Votive Masses: celebrates the mysteries of the Lord or are in honour of the Blessed Virgin Mary or the Angels or Saints. New Masses include the Mercy of God, Our Lord Jesus Christ, the Eternal High Priest, Our Lady, Mother of the Church, The Most Holy Name of Mary, Our Lady, Queen of the Apostles, St John the Baptist and Ss Peter and Paul

- Masses for the Dead: contains the Funeral Mass as well as prayers used on anniversaries and other Masses offered for the faithful departed.

CHAPTER FOUR

FROM LATIN TO THE VERNACULAR
A more detailed account

This chapter outlines the development of the use of the vernacular in our worship. It gives an account of the process of translation and approval, and of those involved.

The use of the vernacular in the liturgy was a lively topic of discussion as the bishops of the world gathered to begin the Second Vatican Council on 11 October 1962. Through extending greatly the use of the Irish and English languages in the celebration of the sacraments, people already knew and accepted the benefit of the liturgy in the vernacular. In the ritual book, *Collectio Rituum*, published in 1960, the sacramental rites, for example Baptism and Marriage, were celebrated mainly in the vernacular. In the discussion at the Vatican Council there was an openness to further extensions.

SECOND VATICAN COUNCIL AND ACTIVE PARTICIPATION

The **Constitution on the Sacred Liturgy, *Sacrosanctum concilium***, was the first document to be discussed at the Second Vatican Council. It was approved in its entirety on 22 November 1963, with only twenty votes against. This date, universally recognised as the date when President John Kennedy was assassinated in Dallas, has also an important Church coincidence. Sixty years previously, on 22 November 1903, Pope Pius X issued *Tra le sollectudini*, an instruction on the restoration of church music. Pope Pius X wrote of the people finding the true Christian spirit 'from its foremost and indispensable fount, which is the active participation in the holy mysteries and in the public and solemn prayer of the Church'. The expression 'active participation' became a key note in the work towards the renewal and reform of the Church's worship. The Constitution on the Sacred Liturgy was formally approved and promulgated on 4 December 1963, its final vote being *placet*/2147, *non placet*/4. The date also has significance as four centuries earlier, at the end of the Council of Trent, the Holy See was given the task of liturgical reform.

Sacrosanctum concilium (SC) spoke strongly of active participation:

> The Church earnestly desires that all the faithful be led to that full, conscious, and active participation in liturgical celebrations called for by the very nature of the liturgy. Such participation by the Christian people as 'a chosen race, a royal priesthood, a holy nation, God's own people' (1 Pet 2:9; see 2:4-5) is their right and duty by reason of their baptism.

> In the reform and promotion of the liturgy, this full and active participation by all the people is the aim to be considered before all else. For it is the primary and indispensable source from which the faithful are to derive the true Christian spirit and therefore pastors must zealously strive in all their pastoral work to achieve such participation by means of the necessary instruction (SC 14).

EXTENDING THE USE OF THE VERNACULAR

Sacrosanctum concilium stated that 'the use of the Latin language is to be preserved in the Latin rites' (SC 36 § 1). 'But since the use of the mother tongue, whether in the Mass, the administration of the sacraments, or other parts of the liturgy, frequently may be of great advantage to the people, the limits of its use may be extended. This will apply in the first place to the readings and instructions and to some prayers and chants, according to the regulations on this matter to be laid down for each case in subsequent chapters' (SC 36 § 2).

These subsequent chapters included the use of the vernacular at Mass: 'This is to apply in the first place to the readings and "the universal prayer", but also, as local conditions may warrant, to those parts belonging to the people.' This was followed by noting the place of Latin: 'steps should be taken enabling the faithful to say or sing together in Latin those parts of the Ordinary of the Mass belonging to them' (SC 54). The vernacular may also be used in administering the sacraments and sacramentals (SC 63). With regard to the Divine Office or the Liturgy of the Hours, clerics are to retain the Latin language but permission could be given for the use of the vernacular (SC 101). Finally, it was acknowledged that Gregorian chant was distinctive of the Roman liturgy and 'other things being equal, it should be given pride of place in liturgical services' (SC 116).

The decision on the extension of the vernacular and the approval of translation was given to 'the competent, territorial authority', that is, the **Episcopal Conference** (SC 36 § 3-4).

in each country e.g. Ireland

Eucharistic Prayer

Tensions existed about the place of Latin and the extension of use of the vernacular. An agency or *Consilium* was established to implement the reform programme of *Sacrosanctum concilium* and by the First Sunday of Lent, 7 March 1965, the vernacular was used at Mass, with the exception of the Roman Canon, which remained in Latin. Soon, all our liturgies would be celebrated in the vernacular, one of the most visible and appreciated fruits of the Second Vatican Council.

ICEL – A UNIFIED APPROACH FOR ENGLISH-SPEAKING COUNTRIES

English speaking

Bishops in countries where English was spoken were conscious of the need to organise what Archbishop Paul J. Hallinan of Atlanta, a prime mover of the idea, called a 'common market' of English liturgical translation. The initial meeting of an Episcopal Committee took place on 17 October 1963, several weeks before the promulgation of *Sacrosanctum concilium*, at the Venerable English College in Rome. Ten Conferences were represented: Australia, Canada, England and Wales, India, Ireland, New Zealand, Pakistan, Scotland, South Africa and the USA. The Philippines was added as a member in 1967 and several other Conferences were to enjoy associate membership. Ireland was represented by the late Archbishop Joseph Walsh of Tuam, who had served as a consultor of the Council's Pontifical Preparatory Commission on the Liturgy. This was the beginning of the **International Commission on English in the Liturgy (ICEL), which** became the mixed commission or agency of the member Conferences for the translation into English of the revised liturgical books. Its secretariat was and remains in Washington, D.C.

Though England and Wales made its own translation of the Missal at first and the books for the Divine Office were translated by a group drawn from Ireland and its neighbouring Conferences, ICEL has provided an English translation of all the revised liturgical books for the English-speaking world.

THE WORK OF TRANSLATION

The story of the Missal has been sketched out in Chapter 2. Taking the material as issued by Rome as the *editio typica*, translation work was done quickly but with great care. There was good collaboration between Rome and the agencies charged with translation into the major languages. The guidelines on translation, known by the French title of the document, *Comme le prévoit*, were issued on 25 January 1969 by the *Consilium*, mentioned above, but working closely in its English edition with ICEL. These were the guidelines that directed ICEL as it worked on the revised Order of Mass published in Latin in 1969, which replaced the interim Order that was issued in 1965. The English translation of the Order of Mass was published in 1970 and was in use from the First Sunday of Lent, 15 February, five years after the first use of the vernacular. For four years ICEL worked on the Roman Missal. The work of editing it for Ireland began in September 1974 and the Missal was published on 7 January 1975 and used throughout the country from 16 March 1975. (These various dates explain how the Roman Missal that has been in use since 1975 is also given the publication date of 1973, when ICEL completed the work of translation, and 1975, when it was published in Ireland).

THE REVISED SACRAMENTARY

No translation is perfect and in time its strengths and weaknesses are discovered. This is true of both the translation we have used since 1975 and the new translation in the new edition of the Missal. In 1982, seven years after the implementation of the Missal, ICEL began a consultation with the Bishops' Conferences on the translation. This was the beginning of a process that would result in a complete revision of the Missal, usually known as the Revised Sacramentary.

ICEL took great care with this revision. The translation work began in late 1987 and was completed in 1998 when the eleven member Bishops' Conferences approved the revision. The background of each Latin text and their translation into other languages were studied, something that was not possible in the early 1970s. But it was more than a revision of the translation. It also included the composition of many new prayer texts, something that ICEL has done with its revision of the funeral rites, the Order of Christian Funerals. This was in accord with ICEL's 1964 mandate: 'to work out a plan for the translation of liturgical texts and the provision of original texts where required in language which would be correct, dignified, intelligible and suitable for recitation and singing …' The work of drafting and re-drafting was carried out with great care and Conferences were informed through progress reports until the new Missal or Revised Sacramentary was issued in eight segments, beginning in 1992. Each segment was subject to the approval by the Bishops' Conferences. The Irish Bishops' Conference, working closely with the neighbouring Conferences of England and Wales and Scotland, submitted a common version of the Missal for the three Conferences in December 1998.

However, the Revised Sacramentary did not receive the approval or *recognitio* of the Congregation for Divine Worship. The Congregation was very critical of ICEL's work, both of the translated texts and the original material composed in English. It became known very soon that the Congregation was also preparing a new instruction giving norms and guidelines for the translation of liturgical books. Furthermore, in the Jubilee Year 2000, Pope John Paul II announced that there would be a new third edition of the Roman Missal.

A NEW INSTRUCTION ON TRANSLATION

┌ See page 61.

The **Instruction**, *Liturgiam authenticam* was published in 2001, coming into effect on 25 April of the same year. As well as norms on translation, it also lays down regulations for commissions such as ICEL. Such a commission is set up by the Congregation at the request of the Bishops' Conferences involved and is governed by statutes approved by the Apostolic See. While the original mandate of ICEL has included the composition of texts in English, the new norms limit its work to the translation of the Latin liturgical books.

THIRD EDITION OF THE LATIN MISSAL

As noted already, the third edition of the Latin Missal was published in 2002, with an amended reprint in 2008. As the official Latin text, serving as the *editio typica*, this is the starting point for the work of translation.

TOWARDS A NEW MISSAL FOR IRELAND

ICEL, through its secretariat based in Washington, D.C., began this work in 2002, first making a draft or base translation of the different parts of the Missal, reviewing it through its own body of consultants, testing it both for its accuracy of translation but also its suitability for proclamation and, in many cases, for singing. The draft text was then reviewed by a small group of experts, the Roman Missal Editorial Committee, to bring a unity of style and language. The final review before the texts were sent to the Bishops' Conferences was made by eleven bishop-members of ICEL. Bishop John McAreavey of Dromore has been the Irish bishop-member since 2002. The texts were issued in twelve segments, between February 2004 and September 2009, firstly as 'green books', that is, in green covers, sent to the Conferences for their comments. In Ireland, as the master copy of each segment was received, it was copied, distributed to each bishop and to the members of the Irish Commission for Liturgy, the primary consultative agency of the Conference. Comments were made by both the bishops and this Commission and forwarded to ICEL. The comments from the various Conferences were evaluated and this led to a revision version of each segment, after review and approval of the bishop-members of ICEL. These were forwarded to the Conferences as 'grey books', because of the colour of the cover, and were subject to a vote of approval, yes or no.

The **Irish Bishops' Conference** received the first segment in 'green book' form in February 2004 and completed its voting of approval on the final 'grey book' segment in October 2009. The text of the Missal was then submitted to the **Congregation for Divine Worship and the Discipline of the Sacraments (CDWDS)** for its review and approval. CDWDS, as it is known since 1975, is made up of two departments joined together into one congregation or dicastery in 1969 and reflected in its title. Its origins go back to the Sacred Congregation of Rites established in 1588. It is the Roman Congregation charged with the regulation and promotion of the liturgy. Among its specific tasks is that of reviewing and approving the translation of liturgical books. In reviewing the translation, the Congregation may make changes to the text. CDWDS gave its approval or *recognitio* for the Roman Missal submitted by the Irish Bishops' Conference in a decree dated 18 June 2010, signed by Cardinal Antonio Cañizares Llovera, its Prefect, and Archbishop J. Augustine Di Noia OP, its Archbishop-Secretary.

VOX CLARA, AN AGENCY TO ASSIST CDWDS

In the work of reviewing the translation of the Missal in English, CDWDS has been assisted by Vox Clara, a committee of senior bishops formed in 2001. It is chaired by Cardinal George Pell of Sydney, Australia, and Bishop Philip Boyce of Raphoe is a member. During its twentieth meeting, on 28 April 2010 a presentation copy of the new English Missal was given to Pope Benedict XVI. Pope Benedict, in thanking the committee, said:

> I welcome the news that the English translation of the Roman Missal will soon be ready for publication, so that the texts you have worked so hard to prepare may be proclaimed in the liturgy that is celebrated across the anglophone world. Through these sacred texts and the actions that accompany them, Christ will be made present and active in the midst of his people. The voice that helped bring these words to birth will have completed its task.

CHALLENGE AND OPPORTUNITY

Pope Benedict went on to speak of 'the task of preparing for the reception of the new translation by clergy and lay faithful'. He said,

> Many will find it hard to adjust to unfamiliar texts after nearly forty years of continuous use of the previous translation. The change will need to be introduced with due sensitivity and the opportunity for catechesis that it presents will need to be firmly grasped. I pray that in this way any risk of confusion or bewilderment will be averted, and the change will serve instead as a springboard for a renewal and a deepening of Eucharistic devotion all over the English-speaking world.

> O God, who in your wonderful providence
> decreed that Christ's Kingdom
> should be extended throughout the earth
> and that all should become partakers
> of his saving redemption;
> grant, we pray, that your Church
> may be the universal sacrament of salvation,
> and that Christ may be revealed to all
> as the hope of the nations and their Saviour.
> Who lives and reigns with you
> in the unity of the Holy Spirit,
> one God, for ever and ever.
> Amen.
>
> *Collect 'For the Church' from the Roman Missal prayed at the end of the presentation of the Missal to Pope Benedict XVI on 28 April 2010*

CHAPTER FIVE

AND WITH YOUR SPIRIT

The Lord be with you.

And with your spir-it.

This is one of the very obvious changes as we use the new edition of the Missal. *Liturgiam authenticam*, the instruction on translation issued in 2001, calls for a translation 'as literal as possible' of the Latin, *Et cum spiritu tuo*, since it is an expression that belongs to the heritage of the ancient Church as well as part of the general human patrimony.

Where does it come from? We look at greetings at the end of four of the letters of St Paul:

> Galatians 6:18: May the grace of our Lord Jesus Christ be with your spirit.
> Philippians 4:23: The grace of the Lord Jesus Christ be with your spirit.
> 2 Timothy 4:22: The Lord be with your spirit.
> Philemon 25: The grace of the Lord Jesus Christ be with your spirit.

Also note some examples of the use of the greeting *Dominus vobiscum* (literally, The Lord with you) as it occurs in the Vulgate or Latin version of the Bible.

In the Book of Ruth, written around 800 BC, the story of Ruth is told. When famine hit Moab, a region east of the Dead Sea now in Jordan, Ruth went with her mother-in-law Naomi to Bethlehem. Ruth suggested that she would go into the fields of Boaz, a wealthy relative of Naomi's late husband, to glean some corn, that is, to obtain what the reapers left for those in need. Boaz greeted the reapers, 'The Lord be with you' (Ruth 2:4). Ruth, whose husband had died, married Boaz, and their son Obed was the grandfather of David.

Other Old Testament references include Azariah greeting Asa, 'The Lord is with you, while you are with him' (2 Chr 15:2). Saul uses the expression speaking to David (1 Sam 17:37). Moses uses it, but in a negative way, addressing the people, 'Do not go up, for the Lord is not with you' (Num 14:42).

The angel Gabriel greeted Mary with the same expression at the annunciation, 'Hail, full of grace, the Lord is with you' (Lk 2:28).

It is easy to see how *Dominus vobiscum* and the greeting of St Paul have evolved into a priest's greeting ('The Lord be with you') and a people's response ('And with your spirit') in our liturgy. We find this in the third and fourth centuries and it has remained with us today.

What does 'your spirit' mean? It is not a reference to the Holy Spirit, though it is spoken by people who live according to that Spirit. It has been said that for St Paul, the spirit is our spiritual part that is 'closest to God, the immediate object of divine influence, and in particular, the receptacle of the Spirit of God'.

St Paul writes about being led by the Spirit, rather than the Law. He is arguing against those in Galatia who had been persuaded of the need to observe the Jewish law and customs. Paul states that Christ has set us free and that it is not a matter of the flesh but of the spirit. Towards the end of his letter he contrasts 'the works of the flesh' and 'the fruit of the spirit', which is 'love, peace, patience, kindness, generosity, faithfulness, gentleness and self-control' (Gal 5:22-23). 'And with your spirit' captures these traits; it is having the spirit or mind of Christ as our guiding light, what guides us through the day, a Christian spirit.

In the fourth and fifth centuries, a new interpretation emerged so that 'spirit' referred to the sacrament of Holy Orders. Preaching on Pentecost towards the end of the fourth century, St John Chrysostom, archbishop of Constantinople, spoke of the people saying 'And with your spirit' to the greeting of the bishop at the beginning of the liturgy, when he stood at the altar and is about 'to offer this awesome sacrifice' as an acknowledgement of 'the grace of the Spirit present and hovering over all things which prepared that mystic sacrifice'. The tradition quickly developed that this response, 'And with your spirit', was only made to a bishop, priest or deacon, that is, someone who was ordained.

Why have we been saying 'And also with you' for nearly forty years? First, English – and Irish – have been exceptions, since most major languages have translated *et cum spiritu tuo* with the equivalent of 'And with your spirit': for example, French: *Et avec votre espirit*; German: *Und mit deinem Geiste*; Spanish: *Y con tu espíritu;* and Italian: *E con il tuo spirito*. It is the way the Book of Common Prayer translated the Latin and still used in the 'traditional language' services – *And with thy spirit*.

Second, there has been a school of thought – and a respectable school – that said that the expression came from within the Hebrew culture and meant something like 'And also with you'. Indeed, the great English translator of the Bible, Ronald Knox in his popular book, *The Mass in Slow Motion*, published in 1948, wrote:

> And then, just to make sure that he is carrying the congregation with him, he says, 'The Lord be with you'. And the server answers, 'And with you likewise' (that is all 'And with thy spirit' means). Priest and people are going about this great business of theirs shoulder to shoulder.

However, the response we will be using, 'And with your spirit', will give us a language that is more elevated and captures our biblical roots, as explained above. Let it be a recognition of the spirit that is among us as Christians, a spirit that we must live, and, in greeting one another, it proclaims the presence of Christ among us.

As well as a formula for the Opening Greeting, the dialogue, 'The Lord be with you' 'And with your spirit' is used at the beginning of the Gospel reading, the Preface Dialogue and the final Blessing at Mass. 'And with your spirit' is also the response to the other Greetings at the beginning of Mass and to 'The peace of the Lord be with you always'.

CHAPTER SIX

THE OPENING GREETING AT MASS

The opening greeting at Mass is taken from the greetings that are found in the writing of St Paul and reflect how the early Christians greeted one another. In their new translation the small changes make the greeting as close and accurate to the biblical reference as possible.

1.
> The grace of our Lord Jesus Christ,
> and the love of God
> and the communion of the Holy Spirit
> be with you all.

This is the last verse of St Paul's second letter to the Corinthians (2 Cor 13:13). 'Communion' translates the Greek word *koinónia* and its Latin translation *communicatio* in both the *Missale Romanum* and the Vulgate, the Latin translation of the Bible. *Koinónia* is a very rich word. Pope John Paul II said '*Koinónia* is a dimension which clothes the very constitution of the Church and every expression of it'. At the beginning of the Jubilee Year of 2000, he said that to make the Church the school and home of this life of communion is the great challenge that faces the Church today.

2.
> Grace to you and peace from God our Father
> and the Lord Jesus Christ.

This is a standard greeting in the letters of St Paul (Rom 1:7, 1 Cor 1:3, 2 Cor 1:2, Eph 1:2, Phil 1:2, 2 Thess 1:2, Philem 1:3). The word order, with the pronoun between the two nouns, follows the Greek, which is also that of the Latin Vulgate version and English translations like the older Douai and King James and the contemporary RSV and NRSV.

The greeting in slightly different forms is found in several other New Testament letters (Col 1:2, 1 Thess 1:1, 1 Pet 1:2, 1 Tim 1:2, 2 Tim 1:2, Tit 1:4, 2 Jn 3, Rev 1:4).

3.
> The Lord be with you.

4.
> Peace be with you.

This is the greeting said by a Bishop and is that of the Risen Lord spoken twice to the frightened disciples when he stood among them on Easter Sunday evening (Jn 20:19, 21). A week later he appeared to them 'and Thomas was with them' and said this greeting (Jn 19:26). When the disciples returned from Emmaus and told their story to the eleven and their companions, the Risen Lord stood among them and said 'Peace be with you' (Lk 24:36).

The people's response to the greeting is 'And with your spirit'.

CHAPTER SEVEN

CONFITEOR

After the greeting, the celebrant invites those present to take part in the Penitential Act, 'Let us acknowledge our sins', which after a brief pause for silence, the entire community carries out through a formula of general confession. The Penitential Act concludes with an absolution, which is not the sacramental formula for penance (GIRM 51). It may be replaced by the blessing and sprinkling of water from time to time on Sundays, especially in Easter time. It is not used when, for example, the reception of the body takes places at the beginning of the Funeral Mass or on Palm Sunday when the blessing and procession of palms takes place.

The Missal offers three options for the Penitential Act:

(i)   the *Confiteor* (I confess), followed by 'Lord, have mercy' (*Kyrie, eleison*)

Originally the *Confiteor* was part of the Pope's private preparation for Mass and seems to have been said silently as he travelled to the place of celebration. It eventually became part of the priest's preparation at the steps of the altar, and in the Missal of 1570 Psalm 42 and the *Confiteor* became his preparation, in dialogue with the server. Now, the Penitential Act is a common acknowledgement of our sinfulness and God's mercy as we prepare to celebrate the sacred mysteries.

The translation of the *Confiteor* in the new edition of the Missal will have a few changes to what we have been saying since 1975. The most obvious will be the use of the words of the old private and devotional translation of the triplet *mea culpa, mea culpa, mea maxima culpa*. It has been retained in the Irish language version, 'trí mo choir féin, trí mo choir féin, trí mo mhórchoir féin'. The translators have been very conscious of the use of triplets in the Latin, not all of which are translated in the 1975 texts. A word not translated, *nimis*, is rendered '(that I have) greatly (sinned)', reflecting the NRSV translation of David's admission of sinning greatly (1 Chr 21:8). The word *ideo*, which leads into the second part of the *Confiteor*, is translated 'therefore', the same way we translate this transition word in the Prefaces to lead us to singing the *Sanctus*.

1975 Text	New Translation
I confess to almighty God	I confess to almighty God
and to you, my brothers and sisters,	and to you, my brothers and sisters,
that I have **sinned through my own fault**	that I have **greatly sinned**
in my thoughts and in my words,	in my thoughts and in my words,
in what I have done,	in what I have done
and in what I have failed to do;	and in what I have failed to do,
	through my fault, through my fault,
	through my most grievous fault;

and I ask blessed Mary ever-Virgin, all the Angels and Saints and you, my brothers and sisters, to pray for me to the Lord our God. May almighty God have mercy on us, forgive us our sins, and bring us to everlasting life. Amen.	**therefore** I ask blessed Mary ever-Virgin, all the Angels and Saints and you, my brothers and sisters, to pray for me to the Lord our God. May almighty God have mercy on us forgive us our sins, and bring us to everlasting life. Amen.

(ii) a simple dialogue, acknowledging our sinfulness and God's mercy, followed by 'Lord, have mercy' (*Kyrie, eleison*)

1975 Text	**New Translation**
Priest: Lord, we have sinned against you: Lord, have mercy. *People:* Lord, have mercy. *Priest:* Lord, show us your mercy and love. *People:* And grant us your salvation.	*Priest:* **Have mercy on us, O Lord.** *People:* **For we have sinned against you.** *Priest:* **Show us, O Lord, your mercy.** *People:* And grant us your salvation.

The translation has been done carefully as some of these phrases come from the Bible. But there are several changes in this short dialogue, including a phrase that the people have said now given to the priest. This, however, follows the Latin text.

(iii) a triplet of invocations with *Kyrie, eleison* (Lord, have mercy), for example:

Priest: You were sent to heal the contrite of heart: Lord, have mercy. *People:* Lord, have mercy. *Priest:* You came to call sinners: Christ, have mercy. *People:* Christ, have mercy. *Priest:* You are seated at the right hand of the Father   to intercede for us: Lord, have mercy. *People:* Lord, have mercy.

'Lord, have mercy' may be sung or said in Greek, *Kyrie, eleison*, reminding us that before Latin became the language of the Mass, the Christian community used Greek. This chant acclaims the Lord's mercy and originally was part of the Prayer of the Faithful before this prayer was omitted from the Mass. 'A Thiarna, deán trócaire' is another option.

CHAPTER EIGHT

GLORIA IN EXCELSIS DEO

'The *Gloria* is a very ancient and venerable hymn in which the Church, gathered together in the Holy Spirit, glorifies and entreats God the Father and the Lamb' (GIRM 53).

The *Gloria,* dating from early times, is regarded as one of *psalmi idiotici,* a private psalm similar to the Biblical psalms. It was originally used – and is still sung – at the office of Orthros, the Byzantine morning prayer. It was included in the Pope's Christmas Mass in the early sixth century and later extended to Mass on Sundays and feasts at which the bishop presided. The hymn was used by priests only at the Easter Vigil. Since the eleventh century it has been included in Sunday (except in Lent and Advent) and feast day Mass, regardless of the rank of the presider. It is also sung on Solemnities and Feasts and at special celebrations of a more solemn character.

The reason for non-inclusion in the Sundays and weekdays of Lent is in keeping with the penitential character of the season, while we don't sing it on Advent Sundays and weekdays because we want to burst into song with the Angelic Hymn (as it is also known) at Christmas.

It is also known as the Greater Doxology (hymn of praise) in contrast to the Lesser Doxology, the *Gloria Patri* or Glory be to the Father.

The *Gloria* is intoned by the priest or, if appropriate, by a cantor or by the choir.

It may, however, be sung by everyone together, or by the people alternately with the choir, or by the choir alone. If not sung, it is to be recited either by all together or by two parts of the congregation responding one to the other.

It is a challenging piece for composers, especially when the setting respects the free-form structure of the text. A music setting can also allow for the hymn to be sung by everyone together or by the people alternately with the choir. Choral settings are also permitted.

The new translation of the text – a good example of a very close following of the Latin – is:

Glory to God in the highest,
and on earth peace to people of good will.

We praise you,
we bless you,
we adore you,
we glorify you,
we give you thanks for your great glory,
Lord God, heavenly King,
O God, almighty Father.

Lord Jesus Christ, Only Begotten Son,
Lord God, Lamb of God, Son of the Father,
you take away the sins of the world,
have mercy on us;
you take away the sins of the world,
receive our prayer;
you are seated at the right hand of the Father,
have mercy on us.

For you alone are the Holy One,
you alone are the Lord,
you alone are the Most High,
Jesus Christ,
with the Holy Spirit,
in the glory of God the Father.
Amen.

There are several changes from the text we have been using. We have used an ecumenical translation published in 1970 by the International Consultation on English Texts that was set up in 1969 to offer common prayer texts to the Churches.

The opening lines are the Angels' song over the shepherds' field from Luke 2:14. The Eastern tradition refers 'favour' and 'good will' to God, giving a translation: 'God's peace and favour to people.' But the Western tradition, following the better Greek original text and the Latin, gives a translation: 'people of good will', which is what is in the new translation.

Then, five verbs as we stand before God in awe and thanksgiving and address God the Father, following the Latin, rather than the shortened translation we have used:

We praise you,
we bless you,
we adore you,
we glorify you,
we give you thanks …

THE NEW MISSAL: EXPLAINING THE CHANGES

In the next section, we address God the Son under five titles:

> Lord Jesus Christ, Only Begotten Son,
> Lord God, Lamb of God, Son of the Father,

Very familiar, except perhaps for 'Only Begotten' translating *Unigenitum*, with the last title leading to John the Baptist's declaration in John 1:29, 'who takes away the sins of the world'. Though the biblical quotation uses the singular 'sin', the new translation, following the Latin plural, has 'sins'. This phrase 'sins of the world' is in the *Gloria* twice; it is in the *Agnus Dei* three times and in the invitation to Holy Communion. In all six places the Latin has the plural as does the new English translation.

There is no change in the final section. Note the repeated 'alone'. What is said of Christ is also said of the Father and the Spirit.

CHAPTER NINE

THE WORD OF THE LORD
The Gospel of the Lord, The Mystery of Faith, The Body of Christ, The Blood of Christ

The Word of the Lord, The Gospel of the Lord, The Mystery of Faith, The Body of Christ, The Blood of Christ – a list of expressions used at Mass and capturing the great moments and movement of the liturgy. Any changes are guided by the Latin and thus additional words in the English are omitted.

The Word of the Lord. At the end of the First and Second Readings, the lector acclaims: 'The Word of the Lord.' The people in responding 'Thanks be to God' are paying reverence to the Word of God they have listened to in faith and with gratitude.

The Gospel of the Lord. At the conclusion of the Gospel, the priest or deacon who has proclaimed it pauses for a moment and then proclaims, 'The Gospel of the Lord' and all respond, 'Praise to you, Lord Jesus Christ'. It may be noted that this proclamation is not a translation of the Latin, which is *Verbum Domini*, like the First and Second Readings, with the people's response, *Laus tibi, Christe* (Praise to you, O Christ). As with the previous expression, omitting the words 'This is …' leaves us with a very simple acknowledgement of what has been proclaimed – the Word of God.

The Mystery of Faith. After the Institution Narrative and Consecration, the priest invites the people to acclaim 'the mystery of faith'. These words had been included in the consecratory words over the wine, perhaps earlier than the seventh century, and with the new Order of Mass in 1970 they became part of the Memorial Acclamation. The Acclamation is sung (or said) by the people; the priest does not join in as he has invited the people and they address Christ, acclaiming his saving death and resurrection.

The Body of Christ. St Augustine said, 'If you receive well you are what you receive … Since you are the body of Christ and his members, it is your mystery that is placed on the Lord's table; it is your mystery that you receive … You hear the words "The Body of Christ", and you answer "Amen". Be, therefore, members of Christ, that your "Amen" may be true … Be what you see and receive what you are.'

The Blood of Christ. GIRM reminds us that it is most desirable that the faithful receive the Lord's Body from hosts consecrated at the same Mass and that they partake of the chalice, 'so that even by means of the signs Communion may stand out more clearly as a participation in the sacrifice actually being celebrated' (85).

These simple phrases are very striking as they express moments in the movement of the liturgy. Some are made simple by omitting English words not found in the Latin. More often, there are more words in the new translation since they are in the Latin. The new translation of the *Orate, fratres* includes words that are in the Latin.

> Pray, brethren (brothers and sisters),
> that my sacrifice and yours
> may be acceptable to God,
> the almighty Father.
>
> May the Lord accept the sacrifice at your hands
> for the praise and glory of his name,
> for our good
> and the good of all his holy Church.

The words 'my sacrifice and yours' are in the Latin but noting that the singular verb *fiat* indicates that a single sacrifice is envisaged. In the response of the people, the word 'holy' is in the Latin but was omitted in the earlier translation.

CHAPTER TEN

THE CREED

The Missal contains two Creeds, the Nicene Creed and the Apostles' Creed

THE NICENE CREED

The long Creed, the one usually said at Mass, is called the Nicene Creed, but as it is associated with two fourth century Councils, it is also known as the Niceno-Constantinopolitan Creed.

A creed was drawn up at the Council of Nicea, now Iznik in western Anatolia, Turkey, famous for its ceramics. This Council was summoned by the Emperor Constantine in 325 to deal with the Arian controversy about the nature of Christ and his relationship to God the Father. The Council of Constantinople took place in 381 and endorsed the Creed. Its creed in its finalised form after the Council of Chalcedon of 451, using the new translation, declares Christ to be:

> the Only Begotten Son of God,
> born of the Father before all ages.
> God from God, Light from Light,
> true God from true God,
> begotten, not made, consubstantial with the Father.

The Nicene Creed was included in the liturgy of Eastern Christians in the sixth century. The practice was adopted in the West, throughout the Carolingian empire, in the ninth century. When the Emperor Henry II went to Rome for his coronation in 1014 he was surprised to see the Creed missing in Mass as celebrated there. Pope Benedict VIII, pope at the time, added it to the Roman Mass. The Nicene Creed remained the only creed used at Mass until the Apostles' Creed was included in the 1975 Missal.

> I believe in one God,
> the Father almighty,
> maker of heaven and earth,
> of all things visible and invisible.

Though the original beginning is 'We believe', both Greek and Latin Christians traditionally begin 'I believe' when reciting the Creed liturgically. It is repeated three more times to help the flow of the text.

'Visible and invisible' is the way NRSV translates Col 1:16. The change has been made because something can be unseen and yet in principle visible (e.g. a remote galaxy) or unseen and entirely invisible (e.g. an angel).

> I believe in one Lord Jesus Christ,
> the Only Begotten Son of God,
> born of the Father before all ages.
> God from God, Light from Light,
> true God from true God,

'Only Begotten' translates *Unigenitum*. It also is used in the Gloria.

> begotten, not made, consubstantial with the Father;
> through him all things were made.

At Nicea the Creed used the Greek *homoousios,* stressing that the Son is of the same essential Being and substance as the Father. The Latin term is *consubstantialis,* hence 'consubstantial' in the new translation to express our faith in the nature of Christ.

> For us men and for our salvation
> he came down from heaven,
> and by the Holy Spirit was incarnate
> of the Virgin Mary,
> and became man.

Some may be surprised by the retention of the word 'men'. The Latin *homo* and its plural *homines* may include females and males. Jesus became man, *homo factus est*. He was incarnate, *propter nos homines*, for our salvation. A point of doctrine is made by a play on the words, *homines* and *homo*, though the word 'men' will still meet with objection.

'Incarnate', like 'consubstantial', are examples of the new translation using time-honoured words that may have become unfamiliar to many today.

> For our sake he was crucified under Pontius Pilate,
> he suffered death and was buried,
> and rose again on the third day
> in accordance with the Scriptures.
> He ascended into heaven
> and is seated at the right hand of the Father.
> He will come again in glory
> to judge the living and the dead
> and his kingdom will have no end.

There is only one change, a change of word order, in the line 'and rose again on the third day'.

> I believe in the Holy Spirit, the Lord, the giver of life,
> who proceeds from the Father and the Son,
> who with the Father and the Son is adored and glorified,
> who has spoken through the prophets.
>
> I believe in one, holy, catholic and apostolic Church.
> I confess one Baptism for the forgiveness of sins
> and I look forward to the resurrection of the dead
> and the life of the world to come. Amen.

Again some minor changes, including the word 'confess' instead of 'acknowledge' (one Baptism).

THE APOSTLES' CREED

The Apostles' Creed is associated with Baptism, and as a personal profession of faith the use of the first person singular is obvious. It is included in the 1975 Missal 'for use where permitted'. In giving permission for its use in Ireland the Congregation for Divine Worship in 1985 approved the request of the bishops as an alternative to the Nicene Creed, though not to its exclusion. The Apostles' Creed is included in the new edition of the Missal as 'the baptismal Symbol of the Roman Church' and its use is mentioned especially during Lent and Easter time.

The translation used in the 1975 Missal is an ecumenical version published in the early 1970s by the International Consultation on English Texts. The new translation has some changes and reads as follows:

> I believe in God,
> the Father almighty,
> Creator of heaven and earth,
> and in Jesus Christ, his only Son, our Lord,
> who was conceived by the Holy Spirit,
> born of the Virgin Mary,
> suffered under Pontius Pilate,
> was crucified, died and was buried;
> he descended into hell;
> on the third day he rose again from the dead;
> he ascended into heaven,
> and is seated at the right hand of God the Father almighty;
> from there he will come to judge the living and the dead.
>
> I believe in the Holy Spirit,
> the holy catholic Church,
> the communion of saints,
> the forgiveness of sins,
> the resurrection of the body,
> and life everlasting. Amen.

The Latin text goes back to the early eighth century but is clearly related to earlier texts. We find a reference to its title as 'Apostles' Creed' in the late fourth century, by which time the legend that it was composed by the twelve apostles was already well established.

CHAPTER ELEVEN

THE EUCHARISTIC PRAYER
The People's Prayer

The Eucharistic Prayer is the centre and summit of the entire celebration of Mass. It begins with the priest's invitation to the people to lift up their hearts to the Lord in prayer and thanksgiving. The whole gathering, joining with the heavenly powers, sings the Sanctus. In the reforms after the Second Vatican Council the Memorial Acclamation, to be sung or said by the people, was added. As the Prayer ends, the praise of God is once more expressed and confirmed by the people's Amen, often called the 'Great Amen'.

PREFACE DIALOGUE

The Dialogue developed from a dialogue at Jewish ritual meals and is found in our liturgy as early as the third and fourth centuries.

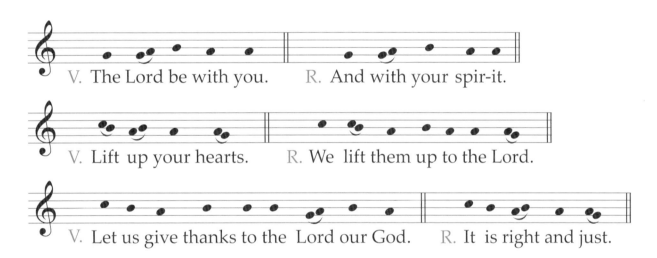

The only change in the Dialogue is the final response which is what is in the Latin and is taken up at the start of the Preface. The second response, 'We lift them up to the Lord', is the translation of *Habemus ad Dominum*. The translation prior to 1975, 'We raise them up to the Lord', is also heard.

SANCTUS

The *Sanctus* was also an early element in the Eucharistic Prayer. It echoes the angelic hymn in Isaiah and the greeting of the crowd as Jesus approached Jerusalem.

Isaiah 6:3

> Holy, holy, holy is the Lord of hosts;
> The whole earth is full of his glory.

Mark 11:9 (see also Mt 21:9, Lk 19:38, Jn 12:13)

> Hosanna!
> Blessed is the one who comes in the name of the Lord!

The only change is the phrase 'Lord God of hosts' instead of 'God of power and might'. 'Hosts' or 'armies' is the usual translation of the Hebrew *Sabaoth*, meaning here the 'heavenly hosts of angels'. The phrase 'God of power and might' captures some of the sense of the power of God. *Hosanna* is a Hebrew and Aramaic word meaning 'Save us!' and thus is an acknowledgement of the One who is Saviour.

> Holy, Holy, Holy Lord God of hosts.
> Heaven and earth are full of your glory.
> Hosanna in the highest.
> Blessed is he who comes in the name of the Lord.
> Hosanna in the highest.

MEMORIAL ACCLAMATION

When the Order of Mass was revised in the light of the Liturgy Constitution of the Second Vatican Council, the words *mystery of faith*, which had been part of the consecratory words over the wine, were removed and placed so as to be the invitation of the Memorial Acclamation. The new translation is simple and straightforward:

The 1975 Missal gave us five acclamations, including *My Lord and My God*, which was included 'for Ireland only'. The acclamations *Christ has died …* and *Dying you destroyed our death …* are inspired by the Latin but they are not strictly translations and, therefore, do not appear in the new edition of the Missal. We may note that *Christ has died …* is different to the new translations where the people acclaim the Mystery of Christ using the personal pronoun, 'We …' or, in the third acclamation, 'us'. Nevertheless, *Christ has died …* has probably been the most popular and most used acclamation. It is used by many other Christian Churches and its composition is often attributed to the late Fr John Hackett, former professor of classics at Maynooth and parish priest of Cappamore, Co. Tipperary who died in 1970.

The new translation, a literal translation of the Latin, adds at the end 'again', which is not in the Latin:

> We proclaim your Death, O Lord,
> and profess your Resurrection
> until you come again.

The second acclamation is:

> When we eat this Bread and drink this Cup,
> we proclaim your Death, O Lord,
> until you come again.

Thus there are two small changes: 'O Lord', translating the Latin *Domine*, replaces 'Lord Jesus'. The final word 'again' replaces 'in glory'. The Latin simply ends *donec venias* (until you come).

The third acclamation, following the Latin, now reads:

> Save us, Saviour of the world,
> for by your Cross and Resurrection
> you have set us free.

AMEN

'Amen' is a Hebrew word that we continue to use in English. The Eucharistic Prayer ends with a doxology or expression of praise which is confirmed and concluded by the people's acclamation, 'Amen'. St Justin Martyr, around the year 150, writes, 'When the prayers and Eucharist are finished, all the people present give their assent with an "Amen!" "Amen" in Hebrew means "So be it!"'

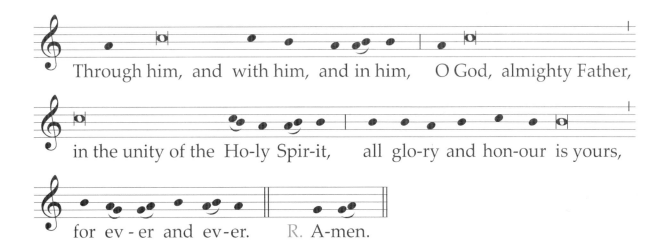

Through him, and with him, and in him, O God, almighty Father,

in the unity of the Ho-ly Spir-it, all glo-ry and hon-our is yours,

for ev-er and ev-er. R. A-men.

CHAPTER TWELVE

THE EUCHARISTIC PRAYER
A new translation

The chief elements making up the Eucharistic Prayer (see GIRM 79) may be highlighted by examples of the texts as in the Missal.

THANKSGIVING

The Eucharistic Prayer is a prayer of thanksgiving and this is expressed especially in the Preface. The priest invites the people: 'Let us give thanks to the Lord our God'. Then he, in the name of all the people, glorifies God the Father and gives thanks for the whole work of salvation or for some special aspect of it that corresponds to the day, feast or season. Common Preface IV reminds us that our praise of God is itself God's gift:

> It is truly right and just, our duty and our salvation,
> always and everywhere to give you thanks,
> Lord, holy Father, almighty and eternal God.
>
> For, although you have no need of our praise,
> yet our thanksgiving is itself your gift,
> since our praises add nothing to your greatness,
> but profit us for salvation,
> through Christ our Lord.
>
> And so, in company with the choirs of Angels,
> we praise you, and with joy we proclaim:
>
> Holy, Holy, Holy Lord God of hosts …

The whole prayer is a prayer of thanksgiving and sanctification, very fully expressed in Eucharistic Prayer IV. This Prayer is composed with its own Preface in which God is praised as the creator, and after the *Sanctus* as the creator of humankind, and then as Father most holy who in the fullness of time sent his Only Begotten Son as our Saviour:

> It is truly right to give you thanks,
> truly just to give you glory, Father most holy,
> for you are the one God living and true,
> existing before all ages and abiding for all eternity,
> dwelling in unapproachable light;
> yet you, who alone are good, the source of life,
> have made all that is,

so that you might fill your creatures with blessings
and bring joy to many of them by the glory of your light.

And so, in your presence are countless hosts of Angels,
who serve you day and night
and, gazing upon the glory of your face,
glorify you without ceasing.
With them we, too, confess your name in exultation,
giving voice to every creature under heaven,
as we acclaim:

Holy, Holy, Holy Lord God of hosts.
Heaven and earth are full of your glory.
Hosanna in the highest.
Blessed is he who comes in the name of the Lord.
Hosanna in the highest.

We give you praise, Father most holy,
for you are great
and you have fashioned all your works
in wisdom and in love.
You formed man in your own image
and entrusted the whole world to his care,
so that in serving you alone, the Creator,
he might have dominion over all creatures.
And when through disobedience he had lost your friendship,
you did not abandon him to the domain of death.
For you came in mercy to the aid of all,
so that those who seek might find you.
Time and again you offered them covenants
and through the prophets
taught them to look forward to salvation.

And you so loved the world, Father most holy,
that in the fullness of time
you sent your Only Begotten Son to be our Saviour.
Made incarnate by the Holy Spirit
and born of the Virgin Mary,
he shared our human nature
in all things but sin.
To the poor he proclaimed the good news of salvation,
to prisoners, freedom,
and to the sorrowful of heart, joy.
To accomplish your plan,
he gave himself up to death,
and, rising from the dead,
he destroyed death and restored life.

This long quotation also reminds us of the need to prepare our reading and our listening of these new translations. The prayers in English are often very long and have many more words as they translate the text and the clauses as they appear in the Latin.

ACCLAMATION

This element is noted in the previous chapter.

EPICLESIS

A chief element of the Eucharistic Prayer is the invocation of the Holy Spirit in the Eucharistic Prayer or the *Epiclesis*. 'Epiclesis: in which, by means of particular invocations, the Church implores the power of the Holy Spirit that the gifts offered by human hands be consecrated, that is, become Christ's Body and Blood, and that the spotless Victim to be received in Communion be for the salvation of those who will partake of it' (GIRM 79). All the new Eucharistic Prayers since the Second Vatican Council have an explicit invocation of the Spirit 'to hallow these gifts of bread and wine, that they may become for us the body and blood of our Lord Jesus Christ' (as we say in the Eucharistic Prayer for Various Needs). The Roman Canon does not have this explicit form but the invocation of the Spirit can be understood within its strong petitionary character, something brought out in the new translation.

In the Second Eucharistic Prayer, the *epiclesis* reads in the old translation:

> Let your Holy Spirit come upon these gifts to make
> them holy,
> so that they may become for us
> the body and blood of our Lord Jesus Christ.

This omits the phrase in the Latin, *Spiritus tui rore*, 'by the dew of your Spirit'. The new translation captures this poetic image. The invocation of the Holy Spirit reads:

> Make holy, therefore, these gifts, we pray,
> by sending down your Spirit upon them like the dewfall,
> so that they may become for us
> the Body and Blood of our Lord, Jesus Christ.

An interesting note given by ICEL reminds us that the dew or dewfall was a vital source of water in a land like Palestine where there are several rainless months. It draws attention to the word 'dew' as a figure of speech in several biblical references. 'Dew' represents abundant fruitfulness (Gen 27:28), refreshment and renewal (Ps 110:3, Hos 14:5), what is beyond human power (Mic 5:7), and a silent coming (2 Sam 17:12). In Is 26:16, we read, 'For your dew is a dew of light, and the earth will give birth to those long dead'. 'Your' dew refers to God and the image seems to foreshadow the resurrection of the dead, with the dew of God's light seeping into the darkness of the underworld.

There is a second *epiclesis* after the institution narrative and consecration when we pray for the Holy Spirit to come down upon those gathered, and we pray for unity and communion. In the Third Eucharistic Prayer we have the memorable phrase, 'one body, one spirit in Christ'. This is retained in the new translation where there are a few changes in the first part of the prayer, a difficult passage for translation. Also we note 'oblation', a word in our traditional Eucharistic language.

> Look, we pray, upon the oblation of your Church
> and, recognising the sacrificial Victim by whose death
> you willed to reconcile us to yourself,
> grant that we, who are nourished
> by the Body and Blood of your Son
> and filled with his Holy Spirit,
> may become one body, one spirit in Christ.

INSTITUTION NARRATIVE AND CONSECRATION

In the Third Eucharistic Prayer we read:

> For on the night he was betrayed
> he himself took bread,
> and, giving you thanks, he said the blessing,
> broke the bread and gave it to his disciples, saying:
>
> TAKE THIS, ALL OF YOU, AND EAT OF IT,
> FOR THIS IS MY BODY,
> WHICH WILL BE GIVEN UP FOR YOU.
>
> In a similar way, when supper was ended,
> he took the chalice,
> and, giving you thanks, he said the blessing,
> and gave the chalice to his disciples, saying:
>
> TAKE THIS, ALL OF YOU, AND DRINK FROM IT,
> FOR THIS IS THE CHALICE OF MY BLOOD,
> THE BLOOD OF THE NEW AND ETERNAL COVENANT,
> WHICH WILL BE POURED OUT FOR YOU AND FOR MANY
> FOR THE FORGIVENESS OF SINS.
> DO THIS IN MEMORY OF ME.

There are some minor changes in the Institution Narrative. The word 'chalice' replaces 'cup'. In the Irish translation we have 'an chailís'. 'Eternal' replaces 'everlasting'. 'Eternal', which is in the Latin, is outside the measure of time while 'everlasting' suggests lasting long in time.

The Latin has always had the words, *pro multis* (literally, 'for many' or 'for the many') and its equivalent is also found in the Anaphoras (Eucharistic Prayers) of the various Eastern Rites. A letter in October 2006 from Cardinal Arinze, the Prefect of CDWDS, called for a more precise rendering of the Latin in the English, that is, 'for many', while acknowledging that 'the formula "for all" would undoubtedly correspond to a correct interpretation of the Lord's intention expressed in the text. It is a dogma of faith that Christ died on the Cross for all men and women (cf. Jn 11:52; 2 Cor 5:14-15; Tit 2:11; 1 Jn 2:2).' Cardinal Arinze wrote, 'The expression "for many", while remaining open to the inclusion of each human person, is reflective also of the fact that this salvation is not brought about in some mechanistic way, without one's willing or participation; rather the believer is invited to accept in faith the gift that is being offered and to receive the supernatural life that is given to those who participate in this mystery, living it out in their lives as well so as to be numbered among the "many" to whom the text refers.'

ANAMNESIS

The Church, fulfilling the Lord's command, keeps the 'anamnesis' or memorial of his Passion, Resurrection and Ascension into heaven, as expressed in the Roman Canon or First Eucharistic Prayer:

> Therefore, O Lord,
> as we celebrate the memorial of the blessed Passion,
> the Resurrection from the dead,
> and the glorious Ascension into heaven
> of Christ, your Son, our Lord,
> we, your servants and your holy people,
> offer to your glorious majesty
> from the gifts that you have given us,
> this pure victim,
> this holy victim,
> this spotless victim,
> the holy Bread of eternal life
> and the Chalice of everlasting salvation.

OFFERING

The Church, and in particular the Church gathered here and now, offers in the Holy Spirit the spotless Victim to the Father. Remembering, the Church offers, as expressed in the Eucharistic Prayer for Masses for Various Needs (The Church on the Path of Unity):

> Therefore, holy Father,
> as we celebrate the memorial of Christ your Son, our Saviour,
> whom you led through his Passion and Death on the Cross
> to the glory of the Resurrection,
> and whom you have seated at your right hand,
> we proclaim the work of your love until he comes again
> and we offer you the Bread of life
> and the Chalice of blessing.

Look with favour on the oblation of your Church,
in which we show forth
the paschal Sacrifice of Christ that has been handed on to us,
and grant that, by the power of the Spirit of your love,
we may be counted now and until the day of eternity
among the members of your Son,
in whose Body and Blood we have communion.

INTERCESSIONS

In union with the entire Church, we pray for all her members, living and dead. In the Funeral Mass, using the Third Eucharistic Prayer, we pray:

May this Sacrifice of our reconciliation,
we pray, O Lord,
advance the peace and salvation of all the world.
Be pleased to confirm in faith and charity
your pilgrim Church on earth,
with your servant N. our Pope and N. our Bishop,
the Order of Bishops, all the clergy,
and the entire people you have gained for your own.

Listen graciously to the prayers of this family,
whom you have summoned before you:
in your compassion, O merciful Father,
gather to yourself all your children
scattered throughout the world.

Remember your servant N.
whom you have called (today)
from this world to yourself.
Grant that he (she) who was united with your Son in a death like his,
may also be one with him in his Resurrection,
when from the earth
he will raise up in the flesh those who have died,
and transform our lowly body
after the pattern of his own glorious body.
To our departed brothers and sisters, too,
and to all who were pleasing to you
at their passing from this life,
give kind admittance to your kingdom.

There we hope to enjoy for ever the fullness of your glory,
when you will wipe away every tear from our eyes.
For seeing you, our God, as you are,
we shall be like you for all the ages
and praise you without end,
through Christ our Lord,
through whom you bestow on the world all that is good.

FINAL DOXOLOGY

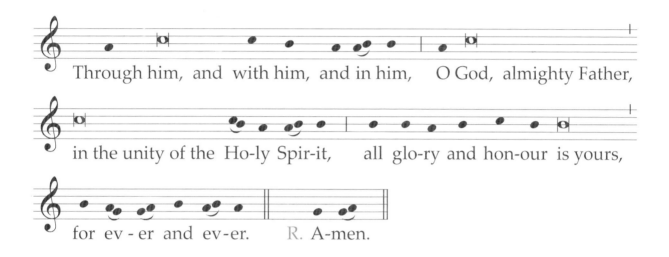

Through him, and with him, and in him, O God, almighty Father,

in the unity of the Ho-ly Spir-it, all glo-ry and hon-our is yours,

for ev - er and ev-er. R. A-men.

CHAPTER THIRTEEN

THE COMMUNION RITE

The Communion Rite consists of the Lord's Prayer, the Rite of Peace, the Fraction or Breaking of the Bread, Communion and the Prayer after Communion.

THE RITE OF PEACE

After the Lord's Prayer at Mass we have a prayer sometimes called a 'prayer for peace'. But the words suggest that it is much more than this. It is the prayer of all who are gathered at Mass though it is said by the celebrant only. Max Thurian, the Taizé theologian, called it the 'ecumenical prayer par excellence'. We pray for peace and unity in the Church and among the whole human family, conscious of our sins and weaknesses. In exchanging a sign of peace we are expressing what Communion is. In that exchange we are challenged to be that Communion.

In the new translation of the new edition of the Missal, we pray:

> Lord Jesus Christ,
> who said to your Apostles,
> Peace I leave you, my peace I give you,
> look not on our sins,
> but on the faith of your Church,
> and graciously grant her peace and unity
> in accordance with your will.
> Who live and reign for ever and ever.
> Amen.

Note the use of the feminine pronoun for the Church. This was avoided in the 1975 Missal but it resonates with the image of the Church as the bride of Christ. When the priest greets us: 'The peace of the Lord be with you always', our response is, as in similar places in the Mass, 'And with your spirit'.

LORD, I AM NOT WORTHY

The invitation to Communion in our Missal begins with the priest taking the host and holding it raised above the paten or above the chalice. The new translation captures the more biblically resonant wording of John 1:29 and Rev 19:9:

> Behold the Lamb of God,
> behold him who takes away the sins of the world.
> Blessed are those called to the supper of the Lamb.

Priest and people respond together:

> Lord, I am not worthy
> that you should enter under my roof,
> but only say the word
> and my soul shall be healed.

Again, this translates fully the Latin, which is the response of the centurion at Capernaum (Mt 8:9), substituting 'my soul' for 'my servant', though in this response, the words 'under my roof' may be confusing if we are unaware of the biblical reference. In Irish, we have the words, 'faoi mo dhíon'.

CALENDAR OF SAINTS FOR IRELAND

The Calendar, as approved in 1998, has one Solemnity (St Patrick) and three Feasts (St Brigid, St Columba (Colum Cille), All the Saints of Ireland). Obligatory Memorials are noted as Obl. Mem. Other observances are Optional Memorials.

JANUARY
3	Saint Munchin, bishop	
15	Saint Ita, virgin	Obl. Mem.
16	Saint Fursa, abbot and missionary	
30	Saint Aidan, bishop	

FEBRUARY
1	SAINT BRIGID, ABBESS, SECONDARY PATRON OF IRELAND	FEAST
7	Saint Mel, bishop	
11	Saint Gobnait, virgin	
17	Saint Fintan, abbot	

MARCH
1	Saint David, bishop	
5	Saint Kieran, bishop	
8	Saint Senan, bishop	
11	Saint Aengus, bishop and abbot	
17	SAINT PATRICK, BISHOP, PRINCIPAL PATRON OF IRELAND	SOLEMNITY
21	Saint Enda, abbot	
24	Saint Macartan, bishop	

APRIL
1	Saint Ceallach (Celsus), bishop
18	Saint Laserian, bishop
27	Saint Asicus, bishop

MAY
4	Saint Conleth, bishop
5	Blessed Edmund Rice, religious
10	Saint Comgall, abbot
15	Saint Carthage, bishop
16	Saint Brendan, abbot

JUNE
3	Saint Kevin, abbot	Obl. Mem.
4	Saint Charles Lwanga & Companions, Martyrs	Obl. Mem.*

* Included as this observance is 3 June on the General Calendar.

6	Saint Jarlath, bishop	
7	Saint Colman, bishop	
9	SAINT COLUMBA (COLUM CILLE), ABBOT AND MISSIONARY, SECONDARY PATRON OF IRELAND	FEAST
14	Saint Davnet, virgin	
20	The Irish Martyrs	Obl. Mem.

JULY

1	Saint Oliver Plunkett, bishop and martyr	Obl. Mem.
6	Saint Moninne, virgin	
7	Saint Maelruain, bishop and abbot	
8	Saint Kilian, bishop and martyr	
24	Saint Declan, bishop	

AUGUST

9	Saint Nathy, bishop	
	Saint Felim, bishop	
12	Saint Muredach, bishop	
	Saint Attracta, virgin	
	Saint Lelia, virgin	
13	Saint Fachtna, bishop	
23	Saint Eugene, bishop	
30	Saint Fiacre, monk	
31	Saint Aidan of Lindisfarne, bishop and missionary	

SEPTEMBER

4	Saint Mac Nissi, bishop	
9	Saint Ciaran, abbot	Obl. Mem.
12	Saint Ailbe, bishop	
23	Saint Eunan (Adomnan), abbot	
25	Saint Finbarr, bishop	

OCTOBER

11	Saint Canice, abbot	
16	Saint Gall, abbot and missionary	
27	Saint Otteran, monk	
29	Saint Colman, bishop	

NOVEMBER

3	Saint Malachy, bishop	Obl. Mem.
6	ALL THE SAINTS OF IRELAND	FEAST
7	Saint Willibrord, bishop and missionary	
14	Saint Laurence O'Toole, bishop	
23	Saint Columban, abbot and missionary	Obl. Mem.
25	Saint Colman, bishop	
27	Saint Fergal, bishop and missionary	

DECEMBER

12	Saint Finnian, bishop	
18	Saint Flannan, bishop	
20	Saint Fachanan, bishop	

FIRST SUNDAY OF ADVENT

Latin Missal
Da, quaesumus, omnipotens Deus,
hanc tuis fidelibus voluntatem,
ut, Christo tuo venienti iustis operibus occurentes,
eius dexterae sociati,
regnum mereantur possidere caeleste.
Per Dominum.

This prayer is found as a Post-Communion Prayer in the Gelasian Sacramentary, a seventh-century Roman collection of prayers, and the Gallican Sacramentary, from Gaul (France), also seventh century. It was placed in the Latin Missal, revised after the Second Vatican Council as the Collect for the First Sunday of Advent. In Advent we pray that we, 'running with good works' to Christ, 'the one coming', may be gathered at his right hand and be worthy to possess the kingdom of heaven. While Latin can put all these ideas into different clauses and make one sentence, it is not easy to do so in English.

Roman Missal 1973/1975
All-powerful God,
increase our strength of will for doing good
that Christ may find an eager welcome at his coming
and call us to his side in the kingdom of heaven,
where he lives and reigns …

The prayer as we have said it since 1975 did not translate all words and phrases or keep the Latin order of clauses; it conveys its general meaning.

Divine Office (1974)
Grant, almighty Father,
that when Christ comes again
we may go out to meet him,
bearing the harvest of good works
achieved by your grace.
We pray that he will receive us into the company of the
saints and call us into the kingdom of heaven.
(We make our prayer) through our Lord Jesus Christ …

The book of the Liturgy of the Hours, which was translated in Britain and Ireland, captures more of the content of the Latin. It helpfully explains that the good works are a harvest to be collected. *Deus* is translated as Father, something which happened often in the 1973 Missal translation. The right hand of Christ is rendered as where the company of saints are.

New edition of the Missal (2010)
Grant your faithful, we pray, almighty God,
the resolve to run forth to meet your Christ
with righteous deeds at his coming,
so that, gathered at his right hand,
they may be worthy to possess the heavenly kingdom.
Through our Lord.

Working with the norms of *Liturgiam authenticam*, this attempts to translate all the words and phrases of the Latin as well as its clause order. 'To run' echoes several references in St Paul (see 1 Cor 9:24-26, Gal 2:2, 5:7, also Heb 12:1). In Advent, while we wait, we also hasten to meet Christ in glory. The prayer also reminds us that those on God's right hand are those who inherit the kingdom (Mt 25:34).

Note the conclusion of the Collects and other prayers, following the Latin and omitting 'We ask this ...' or 'Grant this ...'

LITURGIAM AUTHENTICAM

Liturgiam authenticam, *on Vernacular Languages in the Books of the Roman Liturgy, the fifth Instruction for the Right Implementation of the Constitution on the Sacred Liturgy of the Second Vatican Council, states the norms which guided the translation of the third edition of the* Missale Romanum. *Below is the press statement released on 7 May 2001 and offers a summary of the norms for translation. The Instruction also contains norms for the preparation and publication of liturgical books. The full Instruction is available on www.vatican va.*

In February 1997 the Holy Father asked the Congregation for Divine Worship and the Discipline of the Sacraments to carry forward the process of the liturgical renewal by codifying the conclusions of its work in collaboration with the Bishops over the years regarding the question of the liturgical translations. This matter had been in course, as mentioned, since 1988.

As a result, on 20 March 2001 the Fifth post-Conciliar 'Instruction for the Right Application of the Constitution on the Sacred Liturgy' of the Second Vatican Council, *Liturgiam authenticam,* was approved by the Holy Father in an audience with the Cardinal Secretary of State and on 28 March it was issued by the Congregation for Divine Worship and the Discipline of the Sacraments. It takes effect on 25 April 2001.

The Instruction *Liturgiam authenticam* serves to set forth authoritatively the manner in which the provisions of article 36 of the Liturgy Constitution are to be applied to the vernacular translation of the texts of the Roman Liturgy. That article states:

§ 1. The use of the Latin language is to be preserved in the Latin Rites, while maintaining particular law.

§ 2. However, since the use of the vernacular not infrequently may be of great benefit to the people either in the Mass or in the administration of the Sacraments, or in the other parts of the Liturgy, a wider use may be made of it especially in the readings and instructions [to the people], in certain prayers and sung texts, according to the norms on this matter to be set forth in detail in the chapters following.

§ 3. With due regard for such norms, it pertains to the competent territorial ecclesiastical authority mentioned in article 22, § 2, in consultation, if the case arises, with Bishops of neighboring regions which have the same language, to make decisions regarding whether and to what extent the vernacular language is to be used. Their decisions are to be approved – that is, confirmed – by the Apostolic See.

§ 4. A translation of a Latin text into the vernacular for use in the Liturgy must be approved by the competent territorial ecclesiastical authority mentioned above.

It should be mentioned that there have been a number of legal and other developments in the meantime, among them measures which have further defined the 'competent territorial ecclesiastical authorities' of which the Constitution speaks. In practice these have become what are known as the Bishops' Conferences today.

OVERVIEW

The Fifth Instruction begins by referring to the initiative of the Council and the work of the successive Popes and the Bishops throughout the world, recalling the successes of the liturgical reform, while at the same time noting the continued vigilance needed in order to preserve the identity and unity of the Roman Rite throughout the world. In this regard, the Instruction takes up the observations made in 1988 by Pope John Paul II calling for progress beyond an initial phase to one of improved translations of liturgical texts. Accordingly, *Liturgiam authenticam* offers the Latin Church a new formulation of principles of translation with the benefit of more than thirty years' experience in the use of the vernacular in liturgical celebrations.

Liturgiam authenticam supersedes all norms previously set forth on liturgical translation, with the exception of those in the fourth Instruction *Varietates legitimae,* and specifies that the two Instructions should be read in conjunction with each other. It calls more than once for a new era in translation of liturgical texts.

It should be noted that the new document substitutes for all previous norms while integrating much of their content, drawing them together in a more unified and systematic way, underpinning them with some careful reflection, and linking them to certain related questions that so far have been treated separately. Moreover, it is faced with the task of speaking in a few pages of principles applicable to several hundred languages currently used in liturgical celebration in every part of the world. It does not employ the technical terminology of linguistics or of the human sciences but refers principally to the domain of pastoral experience.

In what follows, the general development of the document is followed, but not always the exact wording or order of points.

Choice of Vernacular Languages

Only the more commonly spoken languages should be employed in the Liturgy, avoiding the introduction of too many languages for liturgical use, which could prove divisive by fragmenting a people into small groups. A number of factors should be kept in mind when choosing a language for liturgical use, such as the number of priests, deacons and lay collaborators at ease in a given tongue, the availability of translators for each language, and the practical possibility, including cost, of producing and publishing accurate translations of the liturgical books.

Dialects which do not have the backing of academic and cultural formation may not be formally accepted as liturgical languages, although they may be used for the Prayer of the Faithful, sung texts or parts of the homily.

The Instruction next gives a careful updated outline of the process to be followed by the Conferences of Bishops in communion with the Holy See in deciding on full or partial introduction into liturgical use of a given language.

The Translation of Liturgical Texts

The heart of the Instruction is a fresh exposition with a reflective tone of principles that should govern the vernacular translation of liturgical texts. From the outset this section stresses the sacred nature of the Liturgy, which the translated texts must carefully safeguard.

The Roman Rite, like all the great historical liturgical families of the Catholic Church, has its own style and structure that must be respected in so far as possible in translation. The Instruction repeats the call of earlier papal documents for an approach to the translation of liturgical texts that sees it not so much a work of creative inventiveness as one of fidelity and exactness in rendering the Latin texts into a vernacular language, with all due consideration for the particular way that each language has of expressing itself. The special needs that must be addressed when making translations intended for newly evangelised territories are mentioned, and the Instruction also discusses the conditions under which more significant adaptations of texts and rites may occur, referring the regulation of these issues to the Instruction *Varietates legitimae.*

Using Other Texts as Aids

The usefulness of consulting ancient source texts is acknowledged and encouraged, though it is noted that the text of the *editio typica,* the official modern Latin edition, is always the point of departure for the translation. When the Latin text employs certain words from other ancient languages (e.g., *alleluia, Amen,* or *Kyrie eleison*), such terms may be retained in their original languages. Liturgical translations are to be made only from the *editio typica* of the Latin and never from other translations in turn. The *Neo-Vulgate,* the current Catholic version of the Latin Bible, should be employed as an auxiliary tool in preparing biblical translations for use in the Liturgy.

Vocabulary

The vocabulary chosen for liturgical translation must be at one and the same time easily comprehensible to ordinary people and also expressive of the dignity and oratorical rhythm of the original: a language of praise and worship which fosters reverence and gratitude in the face of God's glory. The language of these texts is, therefore, not intended primarily as an expression of the inner dispositions of the faithful but rather of God's revealed word and his continual dialogue with his people in history.

Translations must be freed from exaggerated dependence on modern modes of expression and in general from psychologising language. Even forms of speech deemed slightly archaic may on occasion be appropriate to the liturgical vocabulary.

The liturgical texts are neither completely autonomous nor separable from the general context of Christian life. There are in the Liturgy no texts that are intended to promote discriminatory or hostile attitudes to non-Catholic Christians, to the Jewish community or other religions, or which in any way deny universal equality in human dignity. If incorrect interpretation arises, the matter should be clarified, but this is not primarily the business of translations. The homily and catechesis are there to help fill out and explain their meaning and to clarify certain texts.

Gender

Many languages have nouns and pronouns capable of referring to both the masculine and the feminine in a single term. The abandonment of these terms under pressure of criticism on ideological or other grounds is not always wise or necessary nor is it an inevitable part of linguistic development. Traditional collective terms should be retained in instances where their loss would compromise a clear notion of man as a unitary, inclusive and corporate yet truly personal figure, as expressed, for example, by the Hebrew term *adam*, the Greek *anthropos* or the Latin *homo*. Similarly, the expression of such inclusivity may not be achieved by a quasi-mechanical change in grammatical number, or by the creation of pairs of masculine and feminine terms.

The traditional grammatical gender of the persons of the Trinity should be maintained. Expressions such as *Filius hominis* (Son of Man) and *Patres* (fathers) are to be translated with exactitude wherever found in biblical or liturgical texts. The feminine pronoun must be retained in referring to the Church. Kinship terms and the grammatical gender of angels, demons and pagan deities should be translated, and their gender retained, in light of the usage of the original text and of the traditional usage of the modern language in question.

The Translation of a Text

Translations should try not to extend or to restrict the meaning of the original terms, and terms that recall publicity slogans or those that have political, ideological or similar overtones should be avoided. Academic and secular style-books on vernacular composition should not be used uncritically, since the Church has distinctive things to say and a style of expression that is appropriate to them.

Translation is a collaborative effort that should maintain continuity as much as possible between the original and vernacular texts. The translator must possess not only special skills, but also a trust in divine mercy and a spirit of prayer, as well as a readiness to accept review of his work by others. When substantial changes are needed to bring a given liturgical book into conformity with this Instruction, such revisions must be made all at once so as to avoid repeated disturbances or a sense of continual instability in liturgical prayer.

Scriptural Translations

Special consideration is given to the translation of the Scriptures for use in the Liturgy. A version should be developed which is exegetically sound and also suitable for the Liturgy. Such a translation should be used universally within the area of a single Bishops' Conference and be the same for a given passage in all parts of the liturgical books. The aim should be a distinctive sacred style in each language that is consonant, as far as possible, with the established vocabulary of popular Catholic usage and major catechetical texts. All doubtful cases regarding canonicity and the ordering of verses should be resolved by reference to the Neo-Vulgate.

Concrete images found in words referring in figurative language that speaks, for example of the 'finger', the 'hand', the 'face' of God, or of his 'walking', and terms like 'flesh' and the so on, should usually be translated literally and not replaced by abstractions. These are distinctive features of the biblical text that are to be maintained.

Other Liturgical Texts

Norms for the translation of the Bible as used in the Liturgy apply also in general to the translation of liturgical prayers. At the same time, it must be acknowledged that while liturgical prayer is formed by the culture which practices it, it is also formative of culture, so that the relationship is not merely passive. As a result, liturgical language can be expected to diverge from ordinary speech, as well as to reflect its better elements. The ideal is to develop a dignified vernacular fit for worship in a given cultural context.

Liturgical vocabulary must include the major characteristics of the Roman Rite, and should be drawn from patristic sources and harmonised with biblical texts. The vocabulary and usage of the vernacular translation of the *Catechism of the Catholic Church* should be respected as far as this is feasible, and the proper distinctive terms should be used for sacred persons or things, rather than employing the same words as for the persons or things of everyday domestic life.

Syntax, style and literary genre are also key elements to be considered in rendering a faithful translation. The relationship between clauses, especially as expressed through subordination and devices such as parallelism, must be accurately conveyed. Verbs must be translated precisely in respect of person, number and voice, while some latitude will be needed in rendering more complex syntactical structures.

A prime consideration should be the fact that liturgical texts are intended to be publicly proclaimed aloud and even sung.

Particular Types of Texts

Specific norms are then given for the translation of Eucharistic Prayers, the Creed, (which is to be translated in the first person singular: 'I believe …'), and the general ordering and layout of liturgical books and their preliminary decrees and introductory texts. This is followed by a description of the preparation of translations by Bishops' Conferences and the processes to be used for obtaining the approval and confirmation of liturgical texts from the Holy See. The present special requirements of papal approbation for sacramental formulae are reaffirmed, as is the insistence on the desirability of a single translation of the Liturgy, especially the Order of Mass, within each language group.